FACE VALUE

SAVE YOUR MONEY & YOUR SKIN

GREGORY LANDSMAN PHD

Copyright © 2009 Gregory Landsman.

Reprinted 2011, 2016, 2018, 2020, 2022, 2024, 2025

Published in the United States by Hill of Content Publishing

Published in the United Kingdom by Hill of Content Publishing

Published in Australia by Hill of Content Publishing

Published in India by Hill of Content Publishing

Distributed by Etoile International Group. Hong Kong.

hillofcontentpublishing.com

PO Box 24 East Melbourne 8002 Victoria Australia

All rights reserved. No part of this publication may be reproduced, stored in a retrieval system or transmitted in any form by any means without the prior permission of the copyright owner. Enquiries should be made to the publisher. Every effort has been made to ensure that this book is free from error or omissions. However, the Publisher, the Author, the Editor or their respective employees or agents, shall not accept responsibility for injury, loss or damage occasioned to any person acting or refraining from action as a result of material in this book whether or not such injury, loss or damage is in any way due to any negligent act or omission, breach of duty or default on the part of the Publisher, the Author, the Editor, or their respective employees or agents. The Author, the Publisher, the Editor and their respective employees or agents do not accept any responsibility for the actions of any person - actions which are related in any way to information contained in this book.

Author: Landsman, Gregory.

Title: Face Value : Save Your Money & Your Skin / Gregory Landsman.

ISBN: 9780648289210

CONTENTS

LET'S BE HONEST...	1
From the Author	4
THE TRUTH ABOUT HOW SKIN AGES	7
What Makes a Good Moisturiser	11
What's New About This Edition of Face Value	14
Introduction	17
Plant Powered Active Skin Boosters In Your Kitchen	19
Powerful Skin Smoothing Oils For The Skin	22
A Message For The Reader	24

Part I
NIGHT REPAIR SERUMS

Potent Ultra Skin Renewing Night Serum	29
Hydra Nourishing And Toning Eye Serum	31
Face, Neck And Décolleté Moisture Rich Night Serum	33
Skin Energising And Hydrating Night Serum	35
Skin Building And Repair Night Serum	37
Skin Brightening And Tightening Nourishing Night Serum	39

Part II
FACE REJUVENATORS

Skin Enhancing Cleansing Creams	43
Intensifying Skin Toning Lotions	45
Skin Enriching Face Moisturisers	47
Avocado Skin Moisturising And Exfoliation Treatment	49
Peel And Reveal Revitalising Skin Treatment	50
Skin Renewal Face Packs	52

Face Nourishers To Stimulate & Restore Skin Radiance	55
Secrets To Dealing With The Fine Line	57
3 Minute Secret Intensive Skin Revival Facial	60
The Secret To Taking Charge Of Oily Skin	61
Natural Moisture Binding Lip Gloss	63
Revitalising Eye Treatments	65
The Wow Brow Secret	67

Part III
BODY TREATMENTS

Neck Toning Treatments	71
Skin Rejuvenating Soaks	73
Luminous Skin Body Scrubs	75
The Secret To Restoring The Colour Of Your Skin Naturally	77
Restorative Hand Treatments	79
Sunburn Relief Treatments	81
Feet Soothers	83
Secret Teeth Whiteners and Brighteners	85
Secrets To Feeding Your Skin Inside & Out	87

Part IV
HAIR TREATMENTS

Moisture Rich Hair Treatments	91
Skin Conditioning Fine Facial Hair Removal Treatment	94
Secrets To Saying Goodbye To Dandruff	96

Part V
SPOT TREATMENTS

Secrets To Skin Renewal For Problem Spots	101
Secrets To Skin Renewal For Problem Spots	103
Ultra Hydrating Skin Renewal Treatment for Blemishes	105

Part VI
SUPPORTING YOUR SKIN & YOUR WELLBEING

Food Secrets for Radiant Skin	109
Skin Savers	117
The Equality of Beauty Philosophy	120
Beauty Wings	123
As you journey through life...	125
Gregory Landsman's De-Stress & Age Less™ Methodology	127
About The Author Gregory Landsman PhD	129
Connect with Gregory Landsman	131

LET'S BE HONEST...

We live in a world where people are injecting snake venom to freeze expression, using their own blood as a serum, and massaging their skin with snails. Yes, snails.

We are putting bird poop on our faces and calling it luxury. We're burning, freezing, inflaming, inflating, bruising, scraping, and paralysing our skin in the name of a youthful complexion.

And somehow, we've been convinced this is normal.

From vampire facials made of spun plasma drawn from your own arm, to 24-carat gold leaf sheets glued to the skin, to fire facials (where a towel soaked in alcohol is set alight on your face) - and yes, it's as dangerous as it sounds - the beauty industry has slowly crossed the line from science into spectacle.

And all of it — all of it — is being sold to us as self-care.

You may ask, how did we get here? Let's call it what it really is - a billion-dollar con that thrives on insecurity and confusion. It tells us the more painful, expensive, or outrageous the treatment, the more beautiful we'll become. It promises glow and delivers trauma. It sells hope in a syringe and calls it empowerment.

And in the middle of this circus of absurdity, we've forgotten one thing - that your skin doesn't need punishment, it needs nourishment.

While the industry pushes donkey milk facials, electromagnetic zapping, and needles filled with toxins, the most powerful remedies for firming, hydrating, and rejuvenating skin are still the simplest, and they've been sitting in your kitchen all along.

Olive oil. Cucumber. Egg white. Honey. Oatmeal. Aloe. Lemon. Avocado.

These ingredients don't need a celebrity endorsement. They've been quietly, gently, and effectively healing skin for generations. And yes, they're all proven by science.

Packed with antioxidants, essential fatty acids, vitamins A, C, and E, natural enzymes, anti-inflammatory compounds and skin-repairing nutrients, these ingredients have been studied, tested, and proven to support the skin's barrier, reduce inflammation, boost hydration, and restore radiance.

This book, Face Value, is about stripping back the noise and getting honest. It's a reminder that neither your skin, nor your self-worth, require circus tricks or chemical warfare. Nor do not need to spend hundreds to have glowing skin.

The skin is a living, breathing organ that thrives on nourishment, rest, kindness, and natural care.

In these pages, you'll find treatments that hydrate, calm, tighten, brighten, and support your skin, with nothing more than the contents of your pantry and a willingness to care for yourself in a whole new way.

So let's go back to the kitchen...

FROM THE AUTHOR

The simple do-it-yourself plant-powered, active treatments in Face Value target our greatest skin concerns such as reducing fine lines and wrinkles, improving firmness and elasticity and protecting skin from damaging free radicals.

Every formula contains high doses of the most powerful ingredients such as Alpha Hydroxy Acid, Retin A and potent antioxidants used in the most expensive creams on the market. All are touted as anti-aging, stimulating skin cell regeneration and improving the texture of your skin. The good news is that most can be found in your own kitchen!

I have worked across the globe in the fashion and beauty industry for more than 30 years. Dealing with faces every day, I could see that the daily stresses of life show up on our faces, and have a profound effect on the way skin visibly ages, even on those we call supermodels.

With this in mind I put together Face Value; a skincare manual that offers real solutions and real choices that really work! Each of these treatments have been tried and tested by people from the four corners of the world and I have used them in my career for years with great success.

Whether it is a treatment full of firming and plumping hydrators or smoothing exfoliators, these formulas will feed your skin from the outside in, restoring radiance and stimulating collagen production.

So regardless of your age or your lifestyle, the secrets in these chemical free treatments will give you effective skincare solutions to meet your skin's needs. With Face Value you can create a personalised plan for the issues that concern you most; whether it is saying 'bye bye' to age spots, fine lines, blemishes, sun damaged skin or uneven pigmentation.

Without a doubt our faces say so much more about us than what we look like. They are a pure reflection of our health, vitality and spirit. Through my years of experience in the fashion industry I have come to believe that true beauty is based on the principles of Balance, Enthusiasm, Acceptance, Understanding, Trust & You...

B alance in our lives unfolds from the inside out.

E nthusiasm lies within the way we think and feel about ourselves.

A cceptance is the path to making peace with ourselves and others.

U nderstanding ourselves gives us clarity and wisdom to know what we want, and importantly, what we don't.

T rust attunes our heart and mind so we can nurture spontaneity and adventure in our lives, and know that…

Y ou have what it takes to create the life and love you know you deserve and to never settle for anything less.

While Face Value is about learning to nurture your face and your body with great natural products that work, it is also about knowing that the beauty we find outside ourselves is a very small aspect of what lies within.

I have been fortunate enough to cross paths with people who have helped me understand this; each in their own way showing me that the essence of our beauty lies not in our physical characteristics, but in the heart of our character.

While I have seen supermodels in Paris dressed in Chanel and people in India dressed in rags, the one truth that reveals their beauty, regardless of who they are, is the truth of their smile.

So whether you are indulging in a skin rejuvenating bath or giving yourself a three-minute facial – Enjoy! After all, B.E.A.U.T.Y. is about feeling more, healing more, living more and loving more.

> *"You are whole and beautiful for no other reason than you are human."*
>
> Gregory Landsman

THE TRUTH ABOUT HOW SKIN AGES

If you are serious about looking healthier, reducing fine lines and wrinkles, improving skin hydration, and getting a natural glow back then you need to understand how skin stress ages the skin.

SKIN STRESS HAPPENS TO MOST PEOPLE EVERY DAY REGARDLESS OF THEIR SKINCARE ROUTINE

Every day as part of daily life we are exposed to toxins that impact the skin. Skin stress is brought on by the toxins we consume and are exposed to as a result of our lifestyle choices, that dry the skin and cause it to age prematurely. This includes what we eat, how we breathe, the skincare we use, the cosmetics we apply every day, the sugar we consume, the amount of alcohol we drink, whether we smoke, our level of sun exposure, and the stress we carry day-to-day.

When we are feeling stressed, the adrenal glands release the stress hormone known as cortisol. When this happens, sugar levels in the blood naturally increase, and the increased blood sugar promotes 'glycation' in our skin and damages our collagen and elastin - the skin's building blocks that give it structure and keep it firm and elastic. Damaged collagen equals an increase in skin dryness, wrinkles and premature aging.

When cortisol is raging you are aging prematurely! Cortisol decreases our skin's natural production of hyaluronic acid, which acts as a natural moisturiser for our skin. This allows even more hydration to be lost; and when skin is dehydrated, the enzymes in our skin that work to repair the damage don't work as well.

THE SKIN STRESS CYCLE WEAKENS AND AGES THE SKIN

This daily dose of skin stress in so many forms creates a skin stress cycle that weakens skin, compromises skin hydration, creates free radicals and destroys collagen. This results in a sallow dull, dry, complexion, increases fine lines and wrinkles, and ages the skin prematurely.

WE NEED MORE THAN SKINCARE PRODUCTS TO BREAK THE SKIN STRESS CYCLE

It's not enough to just have a good skincare routine and stay out of the sun. Skincare products and creams do not always have the skin building nutrients to counteract skin stress created by daily living, which is why you may be paying good money and doing everything right, but still not getting the results you'd like.

THE SOLUTION TO ENJOYING GLOWING SKIN AT EVERY AGE IS BREAKING THE SKIN STRESS CYCLE

If we want to look as good as we can for as long as we can, we need to break the cycle and counteract daily skin stress, so we can naturally age less! To do this we need to get our skin health functioning at optimal levels, fortifying the body's defence system and simultaneously supporting collagen production.

There are a myriad of things that create skin stress and age the skin prematurely. However, once you understand what creates skin stress, good skincare must incorporate proactive skin stress reduction.

While we all want to age gracefully, there is no harm in giving grace a helping hand. So regardless of how old you are, whether you have just noticed your first line, or they have been etched firmly into your skin for decades, when the skin is stressed we will visibly see signs of premature aging that will show as a loss of skin tone, a dull complexion, skin dryness or fine lines and wrinkles.

My approach is simple, effective and natural, and now in my sixties I have practiced it daily for decades. I will show you how to strengthen your skin, stimulate your skin fitness and elevate your overall wellbeing, so you can feel good and look good.

In Face Value I show you how to:

- Reduce the wrinkle causing hormone;
- Create powerful night serum formulas that will deliver results that rival some of the most expensive ones on the market;
- Fight free radicals that break down collagen;
- Obtain a healthy glow while you sleep;
- Drain toxins and fluid from your face;
- Stimulate and protect collagen and elastin;
- Use specific foods topically to regenerate skin with pure skin lifting vitamins and minerals;
- Protect and revive tired dull skin;
- Plump and smooth out fine lines from the inside out and the outside in; and
- De-stress and age less by breaking the skin stress cycle.

Breaking the skin stress cycle will put back the purity and goodness into your skin that day to day living takes out and show you how to maintain healthy glowing, radiant skin at every age.

WHAT MAKES A GOOD MOISTURISER

Moisturisers usually come in the form of creams and lotions, which are called emollients – substances that soften rough, dry or flaky skin; filling cracks in the skin caused by dryness and dehydration and soothing the skin.

The most commonly used emollients are lotions and creams.

LOTIONS

Lotions are predominantly made up of water with only a small amount of oil content. They are less moisturising than creams, but will always spread easily as they are generally quite thin in their consistency. Most lotions contain preservatives and chemicals and rarely feature any solid nutrients that contribute to the underlying health or strength of the skin's dermis.

CREAMS

Creams are made up of oil and water. This makes them easy to spread on your skin, but they don't have enough oil based ingredients to trap water in the skin. While a cream will always spread easily and feel good when you put it on, this doesn't mean that it is feeding your skin the nutrients it needs or contributing to building the strength of the skin – which is essential to combat skin dryness and make it more robust when exposed to lifestyle factors that dry the skin. It also means that it needs to be constantly reapplied, as the moisturising effect doesn't last.

The reality is that most creams and lotions feel good in the short term, but they are providing short term relief to the symptoms of dry skin, rather than providing a real solution.

OCCLUSIVES AND SLUGGING THE SKIN

Because the uncomfortable symptoms of dry skin are often the result of the moisture skin barrier being compromised, we need to stop the attack by sealing in moisture so the skin can start to repair.

Slugging skin is the practice of covering the skin in an occlusive skin product – one that is oil based and locks in the moisture and hydration in the skin. This improves the skin barrier and helps stop further damage to the skin.

We also need to provide the skin with the skin renewing vitamins and minerals that it needs to restore and repair. So ideally slugging is done with an occlusive formula that is rich in skin nutrients that support the skin to stay healthier and plumper.

Keep in mind that the most effective occlusives are 100% natural and enriched with vitamins that help support skin health. Slugging with creams or formulas that are full of artificial fragrances and preservatives and chemical toxins may increase underlying skin dryness and irritation.

WHAT'S NEW ABOUT THIS EDITION OF FACE VALUE

Since writing Face Value I received an outpouring of emails thanking me for the information. But I would like to thank and congratulate those who read the first edition of Face Value and, in trying something new and different, achieved amazing results; reducing fine lines, improving the texture and firmness of skin and restoring radiance.

The good news is that you discovered you didn't need to make an appointment, leave your home or spend a small fortune to transform and visibly reactivate the health of your skin, as some of the most powerful anti-aging ingredients (including Alpha Hydroxy Acid, Retin A, Vitamin C and potent antioxidants) used in the most expensive creams on the market are found in your own kitchen!

This edition of Face Value has been written in response to thousands of emails asking for night serums, as many of you told me of bathroom cabinets full of potions that haven't delivered what was promised.

So this edition of Face Value features recipes for a number of powerful night serums created from the purest ingredients to repair and rejuvenate skin, even out skin tone and leave your complexion luminous, healthy and hydrated. The nutrients in these serums are easily absorbed, which helps fight free radicals and works to stop the enzymes that destroy collagen, elastin and connective tissue – the elements that keep skin looking vital.

The active ingredients in the serums are highly concentrated with potent antioxidants, skin building vitamins, minerals and essential fatty acids to protect skin cells, stimulate circulation, smooth out fine lines and reduce the visible signs of aging by helping to restore firmness and elasticity to the skin, while boosting hydration. In short their synergistic blend is based on solid science and can achieve the same results as creams that cost up to $1000.

The serums are designed to be used at night as most skin renewal and damage repair occurs while we sleep.

Something that is not commonly known is that as we age the sebaceous glands produce less oil, which makes it harder to keep the skin moist. The night serums are oil based to counteract this. Yet people have been led to believe that oil clogs pores and creates more oil, when in fact this is not the truth. Oil dissolves oil, especially in the pores and allows your skin to function properly.

Many products used on our faces strip the oil from our skin, leaving one of the largest organs of our body to repair itself.

Every time oil is stripped from our skin it overcompensates for the lack of moisture and creates more oil. This is what creates so many skin issues. There is no need to be afraid to apply oil on your skin. Select oils are lubricating, balancing, protecting, revitalising, rejuvenating and strengthening to the skin.

For example Sesame Seed oil is a powerful skin transformer that penetrates the skin quickly, refining the structure of the skin and stimulating cell renewal as it moisturises, strengthens, protects and feeds the skin with rich antioxidants, Vitamins A, B1, B2, B3 and E, it also has a high mineral content, including magnesium, calcium and phosphorus, essential for radiant skin.

Keep in mind that your skin absorbs whatever you put on it and these night serums target our greatest skin concerns with ingredients that strengthen the health of the skin, while enhancing its radiant appearance. The skin smoothing serums are suitable for most skin types and deliver visible results without the premium price. Remember radiant, vital looking skin is created by choice not chance. While nutrition fuels, transforms and can heal our bodies, choosing what we use topically can do the same for our skin.

INTRODUCTION

Research has shown that nutrients can be absorbed effectively through the skin.

This means that your beauty routine will not only give you great skin, but can assist in absorbing some of the necessary nutrients for overall health.

Below is a list outlining some of the benefits of using natural products topically on the skin. Not surprisingly many of these foods contain the key regenerative ingredients found in the most expensive skin creams. These include Alpha Hydroxy Acid, Retin A, powerful antioxidants, collagen producing Vitamin C and skin healing Vitamin E.

There are also a range of ingredients used in this book that are...

- Excellent skin tighteners and toners
- Some of the most effective for rehydrating skin

- Beneficial in restoring the natural pH levels of your skin
- Anti-inflammatory
- Soothing and healing for sore or burnt skin
- Natural cleansers with antibacterial properties
- Natural nerve and muscle relaxants
- Some of the most powerful skin rejuvenating products on record

The even better news is that you can achieve comparable doses of these skin revitalising ingredients more naturally through regular use of the recipes in this book.

This isn't just do it yourself; it's do it yourself for great results!

In the following list of Skin Boosters I explain why they are used in beauty products across the globe and where you can find them in your kitchen...

PLANT POWERED ACTIVE SKIN BOOSTERS IN YOUR KITCHEN

The following skin boosters are some of the most powerful to support hydrated, healthy and radiant skin at any age…

Alpha Hydroxy Acid (AHA) acts as a natural exfoliant that removes dead skin cells and leaves skin healthier and renewed. AHA can be found in a number of foods and plants in different forms including glycolic acid, malic acid, lactic acid and citric acid.

Glycolic Acid is one of the most effective AHAs used for skin exfoliation, oil reduction, collagen building and skin brightening. It can be found in sugar (from sugar cane) and unripened grapes.

Lactic Acid gently exfoliates and softens the skin and can be found in dairy products.

Malic Acid is also good for skin exfoliation and can be found in blackberries, pears, nectarines, bananas, cherries, apples and grapes.

Citric Acid is an antioxidant used for collagen building and skin brightening. Citric Acid is also a beta hydroxy acid which means it has the ability to cut through grease and oil on the skin. Citric Acid can be found in lemons, limes, oranges, pineapples, grapefruits and berries.

Vitamin A (made up of Retinol and Carotene) renews skin through the stimulation of elastin and collagen production, resulting in smoother, more elastic skin. It has also been shown to remove fine lines, help repair sun damaged skin and reduce age spots.

Vitamin A is found in egg yolk, milk and other dairy products, fish, fish oil, sweet potato, carrot, raw spinach, raw tomato, papaya, apricot, broccoli, orange and cantaloupe.

Vitamin C is known to stimulate collagen production, which gives the skin elasticity. It helps neutralise free radical activity, protects against UVA/UVB rays and helps heal scar tissue and bruising. Vitamin C can be found in citrus fruits, peaches, mangos, grapes, strawberries, cranberries, green and red peppers, papaya, pineapple, mustard greens, broccoli, cabbage, spinach, tomatoes, fortified cereals, berries, melons, potatoes, kiwi, guava, peas, sweet potato and parsley.

Vitamin E is known to condition and moisturise the skin, inhibit free radical damage and help heal scars. Vitamin E can be found in wheat germ, nuts, sunflower seeds, vegetable oil (including olive, safflower, sunflower), green leafy vegetables, tomatoes and whole grains.

Vitamin B3 helps regulate oil secretion and decreases a predisposition to blemishes. It can prevent dermatitis and scaly skin and is known as an acne treatment. Vitamin B3 is found in cranberries, tomatoes and green peas. These foods can be used as a pulp to make a mask that can be applied to the face for 20 minutes.

Vitamin B5 helps to increase moisture content in hair and skin. Vitamin B5 is found in cranberries, sunflower seeds, tomatoes, strawberries, yoghurt, whole eggs and winter squash.

Vitamin D has strong moisturising properties and encourages tissue development. Vitamin D can be found in egg yolk, salmon, liver, herring, fortified milk and sunflower oil.

POWERFUL SKIN SMOOTHING OILS FOR THE SKIN

The act of putting what the earth has grown on our skin is one of the most powerful ways to heal, nourish and transform it.

Almond Oil
Almond oil is full of Oleic acid and Vitamin E, which is skin regenerating and reduces the appearance of wrinkles and fine lines. It is enriched with Vitamins A, D and E, and also contains essential minerals such as magnesium and calcium.

Grape Seed Oil
Grape Seed oil is a potent antioxidant which prevents damage to skin cells and is rich in Fatty acids, improving skin smoothness and moisture levels. It is high in Vitamins E and C, together with Beta-Carotene, Omega 6 and 9 and helps the skin with the production of collagen.

Organic Sesame Oil
Sesame oil was used for thousands of years as a healing oil. It absorbs easily into the skin. It is rich in Vitamins A, B1, B2, B3 and E and also has a high mineral content including magnesium, calcium and phosphorus.

Camellia Tea Oil
Camellia Tea oil delivers powerful skin benefits. It is mild on the skin as it contains about 85% oleic acid triglycerides, similar to a person's natural sebum. As a result it is an excellent oil to replenish the natural nutrients of the sebum and smooth out skin.

Rosehip Oil
Rosehip oil contains fatty acids which contribute to healing damaged tissue and skin cell regeneration. It also contains Vitamins A and C, which stimulates collagen and elastin.

Avocado Oil
Avocado oil is a strong antioxidant that boosts the production of collagen and elastin (Vitamin A), and has various B Vitamins including B1 and B2 together with Vitamins D, E and Beta Carotene to nourish skin and enhance tone.

Olive Oil
Olive oil is high in Vitamins E and K (found in green leafy vegetables), and contains high anti-oxidant and anti-inflammatory properties that help counteract exposure to lifestyle toxins. Olive oil can be used topically on the whole body to moisturise and regenerate skin health.

A MESSAGE FOR THE READER

All treatments in this book have no chemicals; no synthetic fragrances, no artificial preservatives and have not been tested on animals.

While all ingredients are skin-friendly, everyone has unique skin that reacts differently. It is recommended with all treatments that a patch test be performed on a small non-sensitive area of skin, such as your hand, prior to using. If redness, a rash or any form of irritation occurs, wash off immediately and discontinue use.

The ingredients listed below are used as a guide only, so feel free to adjust recipes according to your own needs and sensitivities.

As a general rule, ensure that your work area and utensils are clean before preparing any treatments, and that ingredients are fresh and your hands are washed. This will ensure the freshness and quality of each treatment.

Please note that treatments that contain Alpha Hydroxy Acid (AHA) and Retinol (Vitamin A) can cause the skin to be sun sensitive, so always apply sun protection.

Note: if you are allergic to nuts, it may be wise not to use Almond oil in case of any allergic reactions.

PART I

NIGHT REPAIR SERUMS

POTENT ULTRA SKIN RENEWING NIGHT SERUM

The essence of beauty is not something that we find, it is something that we experience through the way we live, love, think and feel.

- Add 3 tablespoons of Almond oil and 1 teaspoon grapefruit juice to an airtight dark glass bottle. Shake well before use.

Tip to increase effectiveness
Apply 2 drops on a damp face. Massage serum onto the face and neck in circular upward motions, giving your face and neck a gentle but firm massage as it tones, strengthens and nourishes the facial muscle fibres.

THE SKIN SECRET:
This serum blend gives your skin incredible radiance. This

formula helps quench dry skin, moisturising it with fatty acids and minerals, while the Almond oil is full of Oleic acid and Vitamin E which is skin regenerating, reducing the appearance of wrinkles and fine lines.

HYDRA NOURISHING AND TONING EYE SERUM

The strength of our beauty comes from celebrating and accepting the differences in ourselves and the differences in others.

- Mix together 2 tablespoons of grape seed oil and 1 tablespoon of cucumber juice. Add to an airtight dark glass bottle. Store in a cool area. Shake well before each use.

Tip to increase effectiveness
With this treatment a little goes a long way. Apply to a damp eye area. Gently massage around the eye area by tapping around the eye with your ring finger, as this stimulates blood circulation and helps drain excess fluids, reducing sagging while nourishing the skin.

THE SKIN SECRET:
This serum is light and effective for the repair of the skin around the eyes. Grape seed oil is a potent antioxidant which prevents damage to skin cells and is rich in Fatty acids, which improves skin smoothness and moisture levels, while the cucumber contains the trace mineral silica that strengthens connective tissue.

This treatment is high in Vitamins E and C, Beta-Carotene, Omega 6 and 9, helping the skin with production of collagen, smoothing fine lines, while leaving the delicate skin around the eye area hydrated, renewed and radiant.

FACE, NECK AND DÉCOLLETÉ MOISTURE RICH NIGHT SERUM

We remain true to our beauty by never forgetting that laughter, fun, tears, and kindness are a large part of what make us beautiful and our lives magical.

- Mix 3 tablespoons of Sesame Seed oil and 1 teaspoon of fresh lemon juice. Add to an airtight dark glass bottle and shake well before each use.

Tip to increase effectiveness
Apply 2-3 drops to damp face, neck and décolleté in upward strokes. The massage stimulates blood circulation and nourishes the tissue by carrying oxygen, which is essential to cell growth and also helps drain excess fluids in the tissue to reduce sagging.

THE SKIN SECRET:
This serum is fast acting. It penetrates the skin quickly,

refining the structure of the skin and stimulating cell renewal as it moisturises, strengthens and feeds the skin.

The Sesame Seed oil is a potent antioxidant that protects the skin from free radical damage and is rich in Vitamins A, B1, B2, B3 and E and has a high content of minerals such as magnesium, calcium and phosphorus. The Alpha Hydroxy Acid and Vitamin C in the lemon gently remove dead skin cells, stimulating collagen and elastin production, while also improving skin elasticity and luminosity.

SKIN ENERGISING AND HYDRATING NIGHT SERUM

When it comes to our beauty the mirror reflects what the mind and heart are full of.

- Finely grate a 2 inch piece of fresh ginger, just enough so that you have about an 1/8 teaspoon of ginger 'juice'. To obtain the juice, squeeze the freshly grated ginger over a small bowl.

- Add 2 teaspoons of Camellia Tea oil and 1 tablespoon of Almond oil to the ginger juice and place the ingredients in an airtight dark glass bottle and shake well before each use.

Tip to increase effectiveness
Apply 2-3 drops onto a damp face and neck. Gently massage the serum into skin with upward strokes as it supports the

skin to remain dewy by stimulating the production of sebum.

THE SKIN SECRET:
This serum regenerates, hydrates and tones your skin. It penetrates deep into the skin to counteract the signs of aging. Camellia Tea oil works in harmony with your skin as it contains around 85% oleic acid triglycerides, which is the same as a person's natural sebum level.

It is an excellent oil to replenish and increase the moisture content in the skin. The ginger's anti-inflammatory properties leave the skin energised, while the Almond oil is enriched with essential minerals such as magnesium and calcium, feeding the skin Vitamin A (stimulates collagen), D and E, and supporting skin to stay strong, smooth and firm, increasing its elasticity and adding lustre to your complexion.

SKIN BUILDING AND REPAIR NIGHT SERUM

Beauty is the silent voice of the heart.
Close your eyes and listen closely to the truth
of what makes you beautiful.

- Mix 2 tablespoons of Avocado oil with 20 drops of Rosehip oil and 1/2 a teaspoon of lime juice.

- Place the ingredients in an airtight dark glass bottle and shake well before each use.

Tip to increase effectiveness
Apply 2-3 drops to a damp face and neck. Massage serum into your skin with upward strokes as it strengthens, nourishes and tones muscle fibres and helps clear dead skin cells.

THE SKIN SECRET:
This rich serum smoothes fine lines, hydrates and repairs the skin. Rosehip oil contains fatty acids that contribute to healing damaged tissue and skin cell regeneration. It also features Vitamins A and C, which stimulate collagen and elastin.

The Avocado oil is a strong antioxidant and boosts the production of collagen and elastin (Vitamin A), it also contains various B Vitamins, Vitamins D and E, and Beta Carotene that nourish skin, enhancing tone and radiance.

SKIN BRIGHTENING AND TIGHTENING NOURISHING NIGHT SERUM

A beauty heart loves people the way they want to be loved and treats people the way they like to be treated.

- Mix 1 teaspoon of fresh lemon juice with 1 teaspoon of fresh potato juice and 2 tablespoons of Almond oil. Add to an airtight, dark glass bottle. Shake well before each use.

Tip to increase effectiveness
Apply 2-3 drops on damp face and neck. Gently massage serum into skin using upward circular motions as this helps minimise fat cells in the subcutaneous tissue, strengthening the muscle fibres and firming the skin.

THE SKIN SECRET:
This serum will leave your skin instantly hydrated, supple

and soft. It is loaded with Alpha Hydroxy Acid, which gently removes dead skin cells and stimulates collagen and elastin.

The Vitamin C in the potato and the enzyme catecholase used in many skin brightening cosmetics are fast acting and work towards repairing uneven skin pigmentation.

The Almond oil is enriched with Vitamins A, D and E, and contains essential minerals such as magnesium and calcium. This treatment penetrates deep into the skin to counteract dullness and uneven skin tone, giving your complexion a healthy boost.

PART II

FACE REJUVENATORS

SKIN ENHANCING CLEANSING CREAMS

*Beauty is like love,
it unfolds from the inside out.*

GLYCERINE CLEANSING CREAM

- Take 3 tablespoons of lemon juice and glycerine
- Mix both ingredients to form a paste.
- Apply evenly to face.

THE SKIN SECRET:
The secret in this treatment is Alpha Hydroxy Acid and Vitamin C to reduce wrinkles, skin aging effects and sun damage.

MILK AND CUMIN CLEANSING CREAM

- Take 2 tablespoons of crushed cumin seeds and half a cup of milk.
- For 20 minutes, slowly heat the milk and cumin seeds in a boiler.
- Turn off heat and cool for one hour.
- Cleansing cream is ready and will last for up to two weeks in the refrigerator.

THE SKIN SECRET:
The secret in this treatment is Alpha Hydroxy Acid (lactic acid), Vitamins A and D – a powerful combination that renews, nourishes and hydrates dry skin.

INTENSIFYING SKIN TONING LOTIONS

Beauty is all that is good that gently enfolds us.

EGG TONING LOTION

- Take 1 egg white, 1 teaspoon of glycerine and lime juice and 1 tablespoon of honey.
- Mix all ingredients to form a cream.
- Apply over the face and neck.
- Wash off with lukewarm water.

THE SKIN SECRET:
The secret in this treatment is Alpha Hydroxy Acid (citric acid used for collagen building), which together with the tightening effects of egg and the presence of honey is a powerful antioxidant that hydrates and calms the skin.

VINEGAR TONING LOTION

- Use an equal mixture of water and vinegar to clean your face.
- Rinse and let face dry to lock in moisture.

THE SKIN SECRET:
This secret will return your skin to its normal pH balance.

SKIN ENRICHING FACE MOISTURISERS

The beauty we search for outside ourselves is a small aspect of what lies within.

PROTEIN ENRICHING MOISTURISER FOR NORMAL TO DRY SKIN

- Take 1 egg yolk and 1 cup of milk.
- Beat egg yolk into milk to form a paste.
- Pour into a bottle and store in the refrigerator.
- Apply to the face regularly.

THE SKIN SECRET:
This secret will tighten your skin while gently exfoliating with Alpha Hydroxy Acid (lactic acid).

MOISTURE MASK FOR ALL SKIN TYPES

- Take 2 teaspoons of milk and 2 tablespoons of honey.
- Mix both ingredients to form a paste.
- Apply to the face and neck and leave on for 15-20 minutes.
- Once dry, wash with lukewarm water.

THE SKIN SECRET:
This secret will gently exfoliate with lactic acid while smoothing, nourishing and hydrating your skin.

AVOCADO SKIN MOISTURISING AND EXFOLIATION TREATMENT

Beauty is like faith, it requires action.

- Wash an avocado and remove the skin.
- Rub the inside of the avocado skin over the face.
- When finished, use the outside of the skin to gently rub the face in circular motions. There is no need to apply pressure as the texture of the avocado skin does all the work.

THE SKIN SECRET:
The secret in this treatment is the avocado skin that stimulates and exfoliates, while deeply moisturising and nurturing the skin with 25 essential nutrients.

The high levels of Vitamins E and C reduce fine lines and enhance overall skin tone.

PEEL AND REVEAL REVITALISING SKIN TREATMENT

Keep your beauty authentic, dance to your own tune, sing your own words and listen to your own story.

- Take 4 tablespoons of caster sugar and mix it in a glass of water.
- Take a clean pastry brush and apply the solution to your neck, face and eye area. Let it dry.
- To remove, dampen two fingers in Olive oil and gently rub in upward circular motions over neck and face. Do not rub around the delicate eye area.
- Rinse the eye area, face and neck afterwards with warm water.

THE SKIN SECRET:
The secret in this treatment is the collagen building glycolic

acid, which gently removes dead skin cells, retexturises and revitalises, revealing fresher radiant skin.

The Olive oil moisturises, smoothes and enhances skin tone with Vitamins E and K, while reducing fine lines.

SKIN RENEWAL FACE PACKS

Carry beauty in your heart and you will always travel lightly.

Homemade face packs not only cleanse the skin, they also maintain the tautness, while removing impurities and dead skin cells. Some face packs you can make easily and use in minutes.

CUCUMBER SKIN RENEWAL FACE PACK FOR OILY SKIN

- Take 1 tablespoon of cucumber juice, 1 tablespoon of lemon juice and half a teaspoon of peppermint extract.
- Mix all the ingredients together and apply to the face.
- Leave on for twenty minutes.
- Wash off with lukewarm water.

THE SKIN SECRET:
This secret cleanses, purifies and detoxifies skin while renewing it with powerful antioxidants, Vitamins A and C, trace minerals and enzymes essential for skin growth and repair.

PAPAYA SKIN RENEWAL FACE PACK FOR NORMAL TO DRY SKIN

- Apply 3 tablespoons of papaya pulp on your face and let it dry.
- Wash off with lukewarm water.
- For oily skin mix with 1 teaspoon of lemon juice.

THE SKIN SECRET:
This secret will renew the skin cells through a gentle but powerful Alpha Hydroxy exfoliation treatment.

TOMATO SKIN RENEWAL FACE PACK FOR ENLARGED PORES

- Take 3 teaspoons of tomato juice and 1 teaspoon of lemon juice and some of the pulp.
- Mix and apply to the face. Leave for 5-10 minutes.
- Wash off with lukewarm water.

THE SKIN SECRET:
This secret boosts your complexion with Vitamins C, E, B3 and B5, and increases moisture as it exfoliates with Alpha Hydroxy Acid.

CARROT SKIN RENEWAL FACE PACK FOR DRY TO NORMAL SKIN

- Take 2 large carrots and 2 tablespoons of honey.
- Cook carrots slowly, then mash or blend in mixer.
- Mix carrots with honey.
- Apply gently to the skin when lukewarm and wait 15 minutes.
- Rinse off with cool water.

THE SKIN SECRET:
This secret is jam-packed with Vitamin A to remove dead skin cells and hydrating elements, which condition and smooth the skin.

FACE NOURISHERS TO STIMULATE & RESTORE SKIN RADIANCE

A face full of beauty is only a heart full of love.

Face nourishers are an effective way to help increase the strength and elasticity of the skin.

PEACH FACE NOURISHER FOR ALL SKIN TYPES

- Take 2 tablespoons of peeled peach, 1 teaspoon of honey, 2 teaspoons of powdered milk and 1 teaspoon of lemon juice.
- Mix powdered milk, honey and peach.
- Apply on to the face and neck. Leave it on for 15 minutes before washing off with lukewarm water and lemon juice. Use cold water to rinse the face.

THE SKIN SECRET:
This secret is a great source of antioxidants to increase the

strength and elasticity of your skin, while exfoliating with three elements including lactic and Alpha Hydroxy Acid.

BANANA FACE NOURISHER TO COUNTERACT BLEMISHES

- Take 1 banana, 1 cup of Olive oil and 2 eggs.
- Beat egg yolks and Olive oil until thoroughly mixed. Mash a ripe banana and add it to the mixture.
- Apply over the face and neck and leave for half an hour. Rinse with cold water.

THE SKIN SECRET:
This secret nourishes your skin with a cocktail of antioxidants, Vitamins A (retinol), D, B5, E and K, antibacterial properties and sulphur to counteract blemishes and help restore collagen.

SECRETS TO DEALING WITH THE FINE LINE

Beauty comes in all shapes, colours and sizes and when we can accept this truth, we will no longer hurt ourselves and others for the simple things that make us human.

Treat fine lines on the face with the following remedies. The nutrients and natural acids in the fruits will help eliminate fine lines and restore skin radiance.

SEEDLESS GRAPE TREATMENT

- Cut green seedless grapes in half and rub gently onto the face wherever there are lines.
- Leave juice on for at least 30 minutes before washing off.

THE SKIN SECRET:
This secret delivers powerful glycolic acid for skin exfoliation, oil reduction and collagen building.

PINEAPPLE TREATMENT

- Peel and slice a pineapple.
- Rub a slice of pineapple over the face or where there are fine lines and leave the juice on for at least 10-20 minutes before washing off with water.
- Refrigerate unused pineapple and use as often as required.

THE SKIN SECRET:
This secret boosts the face with an Alpha Hydroxy Acid treatment that assists in gently removing fine lines.

DEEP ACTIVE RECHARGING TREATMENT FOR PREMATURE AGING

- Take several seedless grapes, cut in half and rub over the entire face. Let dry.
- Mash a quarter of a banana until very creamy and squeeze half a lemon into the paste.
- Mix well, spread over the face and leave for 15-20 minutes before rinsing with warm water, followed by a dash of cold.
- Afterwards apply moisturiser to damp skin.

THE SKIN SECRET:
This secret delivers a powerful skin regeneration treatment through Alpha Hydroxy Acid, Vitamin C and antioxidants, which assist in the stimulation of collagen production.

3 MINUTE SECRET INTENSIVE SKIN REVIVAL FACIAL

There is so much beauty in you... live it!

- Wash face with warm water. Mix 2 teaspoons of Epsom Salts into a deep cleansing cream and 1 teaspoon of lemon juice.
- Massage the mixture onto skin using firm upward strokes, then rinse with cool water.
- Apply moisturiser to damp skin.

THE SKIN SECRET:
This secret renews skin cells with Alpha Hydroxy Acid and magnesium, which relaxes and de-stresses the facial muscles.

THE SECRET TO TAKING CHARGE OF OILY SKIN

*The essence of beauty is similar
to stars in the sky
You don't always see them
but you know they are there.*

FACE CREAM

This recipe is good for removing excess oil on the face and to prevent pimples and acne.

1/3 cup of ripe papaya
3 tsp of oatmeal powder
3 tsp of thickened cream
1 cup honey

- Mix cream in a container.
- Add the ripe papaya and continue stirring with honey.
- Mix thoroughly and add the oatmeal powder. Stir until it turns into a paste.
- Apply to the face and wait for 10-20 minutes.
- Rinse face with lukewarm water.
- Can be used daily or weekly.
- Store in refrigerator.

THE SKIN SECRET:
The secret in this treatment is removing excess oil with Alpha Hydroxy Acids and delivering Vitamins C, D, E and B complex to nurture and soothe the skin.

NATURAL MOISTURE BINDING LIP GLOSS

Self love is the honey we use to sweeten our life.

CRANBERRY LIP GLOSS

- Take 10 to 12 fresh cranberries, 1 tablespoon of Almond oil and 1 teaspoon of honey.
- Place Almond oil and honey in a bowl and microwave for 20-30 seconds.
- Crush the cranberries in a tea strainer over the honey and almond mixture and stir juice into the mixture.
- Pour into an airtight container.

THE SKIN SECRET:
This secret delivers a potent combination of antioxidants, Omega-3, Omega-6, Vitamin E and essential minerals to condition and protect your lips.

HONEY ORANGE LIP BALM

If you like your lip balm to have a thinner, glossier consistency use more Olive oil. If you like a thicker, creamier feel use less.

- Heat 2 tablespoons of chopped beeswax in a double boiler until melted. Remove from heat.
- Slowly pour 2 tablespoons of Olive oil into the beeswax and stir to mix.
- Add 1 tablespoon of honey and 5 drops of orange essential oil. Stir continuously to mix until cool.
- Pour into a clean container and seal.

THE SKIN SECRET:
This secret is high in Vitamins A and C. It regenerates skin, stimulates circulation and hydrates the lips.

REVITALISING EYE TREATMENTS

Beauty is your birth right...claim it.

CHILLED ROSE WATER EYE TREATMENT

- For tired or puffed eyes, place a cotton pad soaked in chilled rose water over the eyes.

THE SKIN SECRET:
The secret in this treatment is the stimulating effect that rosewater has on the skin's blood flow. It tightens pores and balances pH levels.

CUCUMBER EYE TREATMENT

- Take a grated cucumber, by itself or mixed with a

teaspoon of carrot juice, and spread under the eye to reduce black circles or sagging skin.

THE SKIN SECRET:
The secret in this treatment is the high level of Vitamin A, combined with the antioxidants and Vitamin C that regenerates collagen and elastin, essential for skin growth and repair.

UNDER EYE BRIGHTENING TREATMENT

- Run one potato through the food processor or juicer and place the raw potato into two small pieces of cloth, or dip cotton balls in juice.
- Apply directly beneath your eyes. (Don't let the potato juice come into contact with the eye itself.)
- For best results leave on for 30 minutes.
- Wash face with warm water.
- Apply regularly

THE SKIN SECRET:
The secret in potatoes is an enzyme called catecholase, which is used in cosmetics as a skin brightener.

THE WOW BROW SECRET

When it comes to your beauty it makes no difference what people think of you, the difference comes with what you think about yourself.

CASTOR OIL TREATMENT

- Applying Castor oil to your eyebrows and lashes, particularly those that have sparse growth, will make them grow thick and long.

THE SKIN SECRET:
This secret uses Castor oil, which is a triglyceride of fatty acids that stimulate hair growth.

Let me grow gracefully
Let me age gratefully
Give me the strength
To do this beautifully

PART III

BODY TREATMENTS

NECK TONING TREATMENTS

Beauty is a continual process of self discovery and growth.

NECK FIRMING TREATMENT

- To tighten the neck and jaw line, apply a light coating of Castor oil to the neck.
- Place both hands side by side in front of the throat.
- Using your fingers, push the skin on your neck firmly upward to the chin, then outward toward the ears and finally circling down toward your collarbone.
- Repeat this movement three to four times.
- Doing this simple exercise daily should result in a leaner, more toned neck within 4-6 weeks and replace the need to use expensive neck firming creams.

THE SKIN SECRET:

The secret to this treatment is in the motion, which increases skin-firming blood circulation and drains any fluid buildup. The Castor oil delivers triglycerides to the skin consisting of ricinoleic acid, oleic and linoleic acids, effective in the prevention of fine lines.

SKIN REJUVENATING SOAKS

When we accept who we truly are, our hearts open, our spirits are raised and our body is nurtured.

BODY DETOX

- Fill your bathtub with water at a comfortable temperature you enjoy.
- Add 2 cups of Epsom Salts as the water is running. Soak for at least 15 minutes three times a week for best results.
- Optional: add one tablespoon of honey to soften the skin.

THE SKIN SECRET:
This secret restores the natural pH balance in your skin, while the high magnesium content is a natural muscle relaxant that draws out toxins and may assist in lowering

blood pressure, reducing stress, improving sleep and calming the nervous system.

MILK TO SOFTEN AND HYDRATE SKIN

- Pour 3-4 cups of milk, or the equivalent of powdered milk, into your bath water to soften skin.

THE SKIN SECRET:
The milk in this secret softens and soothes the skin due to the presence of lactic acid, a gentle exfoliant which renews and hydrates.

LUMINOUS SKIN BODY SCRUBS

Your heart will tell you the truth of beauty... listen.

EPSOM SALT SPA TREATMENT

This is the same treatment used in many high end spas.

- After showering, massage handfuls of Epsom Salts over wet skin to exfoliate the body.
- Rinse off in warm water.

THE SKIN SECRET:
This secret stimulates the skin and draws toxins from the body.

AVOCADO AND BANANA SCRUB

The pit of the avocado needs to be dried for 3-5 days before it can be ground for this recipe.

- Grind a dried avocado pit until the pieces are very fine (placing it in a sealed plastic bag and hammering it will work, or grind in a blender).
- Mix with a banana and 1 teaspoon of Olive oil to make a thick paste.
- Rub gently over skin (do not use too much pressure, as the pit will naturally exfoliate).
- Rinse off in a warm shower.

THE SKIN SECRET:
This secret hydrates dry skin with natural fatty acids, proteins and Vitamins A, E and C, which stimulates collagen production.

THE SECRET TO RESTORING THE COLOUR OF YOUR SKIN NATURALLY

Beauty is painted with the colours of our ideas, beliefs, acts and thoughts... dismiss any that don't reflect your masterpiece.

These recipes are good to even out skin tone.

LEMON CUCUMBER SKIN BRIGHTENER

- Use a juicer to extract juice from 2 lemons and 1 cucumber. Mix together.
- Apply to the dark spots daily and leave for 30 minutes. Rinse thoroughly with lukewarm water.

THE SKIN SECRET:
This secret is a strong antioxidant formula featuring Vitamins A and C for the growth and repair of skin and is known to even out pigmentation and treat fine lines.

ORANGE PEEL SKIN BRIGHTENER

- Dry a number of orange peels under the sun, or bake in an oven on low. The pieces should be dry enough to be crushed and turned into a powder.
- Add some full cream milk to the powder and mix slowly to create a smooth paste.
- Apply the paste to the skin and leave for 25 minutes then wash off with water.
- Repeat regularly or on alternate days.

THE SKIN SECRET:
This secret contains lactic acid to gently remove dead skin cells, and skin conditioning properties that can even out pigmentation and smooth the surface of the skin.

RESTORATIVE HAND TREATMENTS

Beauty is not reliant on our bone structure but the structure of our thoughts.

SUGAR AND OLIVE OIL HAND TREATMENT

- Take one teaspoon of sugar and one tablespoon of Olive oil.
- Mix and pour over hands. Rub the front and back of hands together and in between fingers.
- Rinse with warm water. Pat dry and gently rub hands together.

THE SKIN SECRET:
This secret will renew the skin surface with glycolic acid and nurtures with Vitamins E and K, while counteracting exposure to different forms of air pollution.

OLIVE OIL AND SALT HAND TREATMENT GLOVES

- Cover hands in Olive oil and salt.
- Cover with plastic 'surgical gloves' from the supermarket and leave on while you wash dishes or do chores.
- Remove gloves and rinse hands well in warm water.

THE SKIN SECRET:
This secret delivers an intensive treatment that will moisturise, regenerate and protect skin with Vitamins E and K.

SUNBURN RELIEF TREATMENTS

It's easy to talk about inner beauty, but it takes real commitment to live it.

MILK TREATMENT

- Dip cotton balls into milk and apply it to sunburned skin.

THE SKIN SECRET:
This secret utilises the renowned qualities of milk. High in Vitamins A and D, milk nourishes and soothes dry, itchy and irritated skin, while reducing redness.

YOGHURT TREATMENT

- Make a paste of barley, turmeric and yoghurt in equal measures.
- Apply generously over the affected area for heat relief.

THE SKIN SECRET:
This secret heals the skin with the natural antibiotic properties of turmeric, combined with the strong antioxidant, anti-inflammatory and moisturising properties of barley and yoghurt.

TEA BATH TREATMENT

- Brew up a large number of tea bags and leave to steep until strong.
- Mix tea in a shallow bath of warm water and soak affected areas until the water cools.

THE SKIN SECRET:
The tannins in tea reduce inflammation, oxygenate the skin and fight free radicals.

FEET SOOTHERS

*There is not a person who walks this earth
that is untouched by beauty.*

SOFTENING FOOT BATHS

- Soften your feet by soaking them in a bathtub or plastic basin with warm water and Epsom Salts for at least 10-15 minutes. The salt will help to smooth your feet, leaving them relaxed and refreshed.

- Alternatively...take 5-6 tablespoons of Epsom Salts, half a cup of white vinegar and 4 litres of warm water. Mix together and soak feet in the solution. Also helps to prevent perspiration and foot odour.

THE SKIN SECRET:
This secret restores the natural pH balance in your skin, while the high magnesium content is a natural muscle relaxant that draws out toxins and may assist in lowering blood pressure, reducing stress, improving sleep and calming the nervous system.

VASELINE AND ESSENTIAL OIL FOOT TREATMENT

- Rub a few drops of your favourite essential oil on your feet. Before going to bed at night, spread Vaseline on dry feet and put on a pair of thick socks. When you wake up in the morning your feet will be soft, smooth and nourished.

THE SKIN SECRET:
This secret features glycerin which replicates the skin's own natural moisturising ability.

SECRET TEETH WHITENERS AND BRIGHTENERS

You can find beauty in the words of a poet, the colour of a rose and in the smile of a stranger.

These homemade recipes remove plaque, keep gums healthy and brighten teeth...

BAKING SODA TEETH WHITENER AND BRIGHTENER

- Take 3 teaspoons of baking soda and 1½ teaspoons of table salt.
- Mix well and use as tooth powder.
- Brush in a gentle circular motion.
- After two minutes rinse as normal.

THE SECRET:
The secret to baking soda treatments on the teeth is its ability to polish effectively without scratching the tooth surface.

LEMON TEETH WHITENER AND BRIGHTENER

- Take 2 teaspoons of lemon juice and 2 teaspoons of salt.
- Make a paste and use on discoloured teeth.
- Brush this on your teeth using gentle circular motions.
- After two minutes rinse as normal.
- Use regularly.

THE SECRET:
This secret will remove stains and is a potent antiseptic.

SECRETS TO FEEDING YOUR SKIN INSIDE & OUT

As human beings we all have one thing in common, the ability to feel beautiful.

SUGAR EXFOLIATOR

- Mix sugar with some oil or water, rub on to your skin gently and rinse.
- Remember to rinse the tub or shower afterwards.

THE SKIN SECRET:
The secret is that sugar is a great exfoliator loaded with glycolic acid and will leave the skin smoother and brighter.

CORNSTARCH INSTEAD OF BABY POWDER

- Sprinkle where you would baby powder.
- If you'd like a little fragrance, spray your favourite perfume on the cornstarch before applying.

THE SKIN SECRET:
The secret of cornstarch is that it helps stop perspiration, softens skin and relieves chafing.

TEA BAGS FOR PUFFY EYES

- Tea can be used on under-eye circles or bags by wetting tea bags with warm water and placing over closed eyes for 15 minutes.

THE SKIN SECRET:
The secret in tea is the tannins which reduce swelling.

PART IV

HAIR TREATMENTS

MOISTURE RICH HAIR TREATMENTS

Your Beauty is an adventure... Explore it.

ALOE VERA CONDITIONER TO REVITALISE NORMAL TO DRY HAIR

- Take a large leaf from the aloe vera plant and squeeze the gel into a cup of Olive oil.
- Mix well and massage into scalp and hair.
- Wash off with lukewarm water.

THE SKIN SECRET:
The secret to this treatment lies in the healing Vitamins A, C, E, B and K.

MAYONNAISE HAIR CONDITIONER TO REVITALISE NORMAL HAIR

- Use ½ a cup of mayonnaise and mix in 2 teaspoons of apple cider vinegar, leave on for 15 minutes, then rinse well.

THE SECRET:
This secret delivers proteins and Vitamins A, B5 and D which help to increase the moisture content in hair.

APPLE CIDER VINEGAR RINSE TO REVITALISE OILY HAIR

- Use apple cider vinegar as a rinse before you shampoo.

THE SKIN SECRET:
The secret to apple cider vinegar is that it helps remove excess oil and product residue from hair.

THE SECRET IN OLIVE OIL TO SOFTEN, MOISTURISE AND SHINE

- Olive oil can be used as a conditioner or hot oil treatment for hair, or to moisturise and soften skin. It can also soften cuticles and strengthen nails, and may be used as an effective make-up remover.

THE SKIN SECRET:
The secret of Olive oil is that it is high in Vitamins E and K and is a multi-purpose beauty tool.

SKIN CONDITIONING FINE FACIAL HAIR REMOVAL TREATMENT

Loving who you are is not a guarantee for a problem free life, but it is a guarantee for a happier one.

SKIN CONDITIONING FINE FACIAL HAIR REMOVAL

- Take 1 egg white, 4 tablespoons of castor sugar and 1-2 teaspoons of corn flour.
- Blend the egg white with the sugar and add the corn flour until it becomes a sticky paste.
- Apply the mixture to your face.
- When it dries, gently remove from the face by rubbing in small circular motions. Rinse face with warm water.
- Repeat two to three times a week.

THE SKIN SECRET:
This secret features glycolic acid, one of the most powerful Alpha Hydroxy Acids that penetrates the skin and renews skin cells, while removing fine facial hair.

SECRETS TO SAYING GOODBYE TO DANDRUFF

When it comes to your beauty never under estimate your heart's ability to heal it and feel it.

LEMON SCALP TREATMENT

- Take 7 tablespoons of lemon juice and 1 cup of boiled water.
- Mix the ingredients together and apply it to your head when cool.
- Leave for up to an hour then wash off.

THE SKIN SECRET:
This secret utilises Alpha Hydroxy Acid and the antibacterial qualities of lemons to remove dead skin cells and cleanse the scalp.

EGG SCALP TREATMENT

- Take the white of 1 egg and 1 tablespoon of lemon juice.
- Beat the egg white and mix in lemon juice.
- Apply to scalp and leave to soak for up to an hour before shampooing your hair.

THE SKIN SECRET:
This secret combines the tightening properties of egg with the antibacterial properties of lemon to clean, exfoliate and boost the health of the scalp.

VINEGAR SCALP TREATMENT

- Take 3 tablespoons of white or brown vinegar and a litre of water.
- Mix the vinegar in water and after shampooing wash your hair with this mixture.
- Rinse thoroughly.

THE SKIN SECRET:
This secret conditions the scalp and restores the pH balance to reduce dryness, itching and flaking.

Allow me to know the beauty that shines within me
Let it shine outwardly as I go about my day to day business
Allow me to feel the fullness of it
To taste the life enhancing sweetness it brings
So I can share it generously
Care for it kindly
And commit to it consciously
Knowing I can't be all things to all people
I can just be myself

PART V

SPOT TREATMENTS

SECRETS TO SKIN RENEWAL FOR PROBLEM SPOTS

A beautiful life does not depend on what we have on the outside, but on who we are on the inside.

HONEY TREATMENT

- Warm a little honey and apply to trouble spots. Wash off after 10-15 minutes. Apply regularly.

THE SKIN SECRET:
The secret in honey is its high Vitamin C, D, E and B complex content and its antiseptic properties, which have a healing effect on the skin.

BICARB TREATMENT

- Take 2 teaspoons of soda bicarbonate.
- Add this to 3 cups of boiled water.
- Steam a towel in this mixture and place a warm, moist towel over face.
- Repeat this morning and night.

THE SKIN SECRET:
The secret in this treatment is the acid neutralising properties.

SECRETS TO SKIN RENEWAL FOR PROBLEM SPOTS

It is our thoughts, beliefs and actions that are not only responsible for creating beauty, but sustaining it.

LIME JUICE TREATMENT

- Take 1 teaspoon of lime juice and mix it with 1 teaspoon of powdered cinnamon.
- Apply it at bedtime and wash it off in the morning.

THE SKIN SECRET:
The secret in this treatment is the Alpha Hydroxy Acid and the high antioxidant and antimicrobial properties of cinnamon.

LEMON TREATMENT

- Rub a fresh slice of lemon over areas with blackheads.
- It will open the pores and dry the problem areas.
- Apply regularly.

THE SKIN SECRET:
The secrets in this treatment are the antiseptic and citric acid skin rejuvenating properties of the lemon.

ULTRA HYDRATING SKIN RENEWAL TREATMENT FOR BLEMISHES

Never let a day pass when you do not acknowledge your beauty.

HYDRATING FACIAL PASTE

- Make a paste by mixing 1 teaspoon of milk powder with 1 teaspoon of egg white and 1 teaspoon of lemon juice. Optional - add 1 drop of lavender essential oil.
- Mix the ingredients thoroughly and apply generously to the face and neck. Do not apply to broken or damaged skin.
- Leave for 20-30 minutes, wash with lukewarm water and apply moisturiser onto damp face.

THE SKIN SECRET:
The skin renewal face paste removes dead skin and reduces blemishes.
It exfoliates with Alpha Hydroxy Acid while stimulating the growth of new skin cells, tightening, hydrating and balancing the skin.

- Alternatively, use a mixture of half apple cider vinegar and half cold water, which works as an astringent. This mixture can also be used as a cooling face treatment in hot weather if placed in the refrigerator.

THE SKIN SECRET:
This secret balances the pH level of your skin while giving your skin a strong dose of collagen producing Vitamin C.

PART VI

SUPPORTING YOUR SKIN & YOUR WELLBEING

FOOD SECRETS FOR RADIANT SKIN

What you put on the inside shows up on the outside.

Aloe Vera
Aloe Vera is moisturising and soothing to the skin and regenerates healthy skin cells. It contains Vitamins C, A, E and B and a series of minerals, enzymes and amino acids which are known to be anti-inflammatory.

Apple cider vinegar
Apple cider vinegar keeps skin supple. It's heavy concentration of enzymes helps peel off dead skin cells. Use as an astringent on oily skin.

Avocado
The oil in avocado tightens the skin and penetrates the layers to the deepest level. It is good for reducing fine lines and enhancing overall skin tone. Avocado contains more than 25 essential nutrients and Vitamins including high levels of Vitamins E and C, which stimulate collagen production.

Baking Soda
Baking soda is a natural exfoliant, neutraliser and skin soother.

Banana
The antioxidants and nutrients in bananas help to restore collagen in your skin. They also have antibacterial properties and can be applied to the face mashed with lemon (stops the banana going brown) or with yoghurt, honey, egg or milk for a range of benefits that assist in maintaining the health of the skin.

Barley
Barley is full of antioxidants and enzymes together with Vitamins A, B, C and E. It helps elasticity in the skin and is both regenerative and moisturising.

Carrots
Carrots are an excellent source of Vitamin A which is essential in the maintenance of healthy skin and hair, as well as Coenzyme Q10 (also found in many high quality face creams).

Citrus Fruit

Citrus fruits contain Vitamin C (collagen building) which helps neutralise free radical activity and most importantly promote collagen synthesis – the key to skin remaining healthy and elastic.

Cucumber

Cucumber contains Vitamins A and C (collagen building) and is a strong antioxidant with a number of trace minerals and enzymes essential for skin growth and repair. It is a good source of silica, a trace mineral that contributes to the strength of connective tissue. Cucumber is immediately effective on puffy eyes, sunburn or as a tonic for the whole face.

Eggs

Eggs contain Vitamins A, B5 and D, and proteins that when applied to the face have a tightening and constricting effect on the pores. When egg whites are used as a mask they also remove dead skin cells. Used as a hair rinse, the proteins in the eggs condition the hair follicles leaving them smoother and shinier.

Epsom Salts

Epsom salts or Magnesium Sulphate is a long time remedy that has a multitude of benefits when applied topically or used for soaking.

Epsom salts have a high magnesium content and as such is a natural muscle relaxant that can assist in lowering blood pressure, reducing stress, improving sleep and calming the nervous system. In a bath the salts draw toxins through the water and absorb the nutrients through the skin. Epsom Salts are associated with helping back pain and aching limbs and also treating cold and congestion through the release of toxins.

Grapes
Grapes are high in AHA (skin renewal) and Vitamin C (collagen building) so they are powerful for use as a skin exfoliant, for oil reduction on the skin and skin brightening.

Honey
Honey both attracts and retains moisture and is soothing and nourishing to the skin. It contains a natural exfoliant and is hydrating and calming to sore or irritated skin. Honey can be used for all over body nourishment in a range of treatments.

Lemon
Lemons are rich in AHA and Vitamin C (collagen building) and a range of nutrients that has ensured its use as a rejuvenating beauty product for hundreds of years. Its versatility as a topical ingredient means it can be used in cleansers, toners, skin brighteners, face masks and scrubs. It is naturally antiseptic and has been used successfully to treat fine lines, scars and pigmentation of every kind.

Milk
Milk and yoghurt soften and soothe the skin because of the presence of lactic acid (AHA), a gentle exfoliant which renews and hydrates skin. High in Vitamins A and D, milk

nourishes and soothes dry, itchy and irritated skin, holding natural properties that calm irritation and reduce redness.

Oatmeal
Oatmeal is appropriate for dry and sensitive skin acting as both an exfoliator and moisturiser.

Olive Oil
Olive oil is high in Vitamin E and Vitamin K (found in green leafy vegetables), and contains high anti-oxidant and anti-inflammatory properties that help counteract exposure to pollution, smoke and alcohol. Olive oil is rich in its nutrient value and can be used topically on the whole body to moisturise and regenerate.

Orange
Orange is high in Vitamins A and C (collagen building) and of great benefit to all skin types via its regenerative skin properties. Orange stimulates circulation and the release of toxins from the skin.

Papaya
Papaya is high in AHA that removes the top layer of dead cells and helps regenerate fresh new skin. It also contains Vitamins C (collagen building), E and K which support overall skin health.

Peach
Peach is a great source of antioxidants that help protect your skin from UV rays. Research has shown that nutrients from

topically applied juice benefit the strength and elasticity of skin.

Pineapple
Pineapple is a citrus fruit (Vitamin C – collagen building) which contains high levels of AHA, has a hydrating effect on the skin and is also anti-inflammatory meaning the overall result is one that promotes clearer looking skin.

Potato
Potatoes contain Vitamins C (collagen building) and B and minerals such as potassium, magnesium, phosphorus and zinc – all of which are good for the skin. Potato juice is excellent in skin packs and can assist in curing pimples and spots on the skin. It can also provide immediate relief from burns if placed directly on the area. Potatoes are also a skin cleanser and natural skin brightener.

Rose Water
Rose Water stimulates skin, balances pH levels, tightens pores and increases blood flow. It is antibacterial and appropriate for dry and oily skin.

Sugar
Sugar contains glycolic acid that is part of the AHA family, which helps break down dead skin cells leaving skin renewed and revitalised. Sugar can be applied topically to the face or the whole body as a scrub that hydrates skin without clogging pores. Can also be used as a one-minute manicure or pedicure.

Sunflower Oil

Sunflower oil is a superb source of nutrients for the skin, containing Vitamins A, D and E. Vitamin E is known for its anti-inflammatory and anti-oxidant properties and is often used to heal scar tissue (and fine lines on the face which are really just small scars caused by damage to the skin).

Tea

When applied topically the tannins in tea reduce inflammation. Tea is known for putting oxygen into the skin and fighting free radicals that are destructive.

Tomatoes

Tomatoes are rich in Vitamin A, Vitamin C (collagen building), and potassium, essential for fresh glowing skin.

Turmeric

Turmeric is a natural antibiotic, a strong antioxidant and anti-inflammatory, and acknowledged as a potent anti-aging ingredient.

Vegetable Oils

Oils such as Apricot Kernel, Avocado, Almond, Peach Kernel, Jojoba, Sunflower, Sesame, Olive or Soybean are all rich in unsaturated Fatty Acids, vitamins and minerals that are essential to maintenance of moisture levels in the skin.

Vinegar

Vinegar can help restore the natural pH balance in your skin which assists with dryness, itching and flaking. It can be used as a cleanser and toner for your skin when mixed with water.

Watermelon
Watermelon is high in the super antioxidant lycopene and Vitamins C (collagen building), A and B, which keep the skin fresh, radiant and hydrated. The natural acids act as an exfoliant which are good for healing blemishes.

Yoghurt
Yoghurt contains AHA (skin renewal), Vitamins A and B5 and will act as a gentle exfoliant that increases the moisture content in skin and hair. It will also cool and soothe irritated skin.

SKIN SAVERS

Sunscreen Saver
Apply sunscreen when you go in the sun.

Rinse Well
Ensure you rinse your cleanser well, as any traces left on the face can dry the skin and cause it to age prematurely. Avoid hot water as it strips the oil from the face and is drying to the complexion.

Add Humidity
Spending long hours in air-conditioned environments can leave our skin feeling dehydrated, accelerating aging. A humidifier in your environment to help retain skin moisture.

Let It Go
Aging is a part of life, but habits like smoking and alcohol deplete the skin of nutrients, breaking down elasticity and inducing wrinkles and premature aging.

Choose Carefully
While many creams state they are loaded with collagen, the molecules are too large to penetrate the skin making it useless.

Nature's Way
There are no skin moisturisers and anti-aging creams that can benefit your skin the way pure natural ingredients can.

Sleep It Off
It is essential to have enough sleep at night to retain healthy skin as stress affects the skin over time.

Drink Up
Water makes up fifty to seventy per cent of our body weight and we eliminate two to three litres a day. Drink a minimum of eight glasses of water a day to stay hydrated.

Start The Day
Start and end the day with a mini detox for the liver. Drinking a glass of warm water with the juice of some lemon in it is a great skin tonic. The water helps remove and release the toxins, which lessens the load on your body to eliminate them.

A Cup Of Tea
Drink green tea regularly. It is a powerful skin drink and adding lemon helps you absorb more powerful antioxidants.

Exfoliate
Exfoliating regularly allows your moisturiser to be more effective as it removes dead skin cells and supports the skin to absorb them easily. Do not over exfoliate, once or twice a week is sufficient.

Cleanse In Moderation
Cleansing helps remove dirt from skin that causes aging, but be mindful when cleansing to avoid soaps and detergents with strong chemicals that strip natural oils and to cleanse in moderation.

Eat Up
Ensure you eat a diet that is rich in vitamins and minerals to strengthen and protect the collagen in your skin (See Face Food). Ensure you include fish oil in your diet at least twice a week as it is essential for overall health and glowing healthy skin.

Exercise Your Face Not just Your Body
It is important to exercise the body as it increases blood flow to the skin and gives it a fit and healthy glow. The face is just as important and with certain exercises you stimulate collagen, and smooth out fine lines. (See Face Fitness.)

THE EQUALITY OF BEAUTY PHILOSOPHY

Balance
Enthusiasm
Acceptance
Understanding
Trust
and You...

are the keys to a good life.

*E*veryday we are bombarded with a concept of beauty where flawless, 'poreless', wrinkle-free skin is shown as the perfect ideal. The myriad of unrealistic physical standards have created untold stress and left people questioning themselves and their beauty - Young enough, pretty enough, thin enough - ENOUGH ALREADY!

These six keys support you to take the stress out of beauty.

They are a testament to the truth of beauty and a celebration of beauty in its truest sense.

THE GREGORY LANDSMAN BEAUTY MANIFESTO
A Ritual for Skin, Soul and Self

Today, I return to myself.
Not to a younger version, not to a perfect image,
But to the quiet, powerful beauty that lives in my bones.

I will live with **BALANCE**,
Honouring the rhythm of my body,
Feeding it gently, hydrating it deeply,
Resting when it needs rest, moving when it needs motion.
Because true beauty lives in harmony, not hustle.

I will greet this day with **ENTHUSIASM**,
Not for flawless skin, but for a radiant life.
For the joy in nourishing what I already have,
And for the glow that comes from laughter,
breath, and purpose.

I will walk in **ACCEPTANCE**,
Of the lines, the softness, the changes.
They are not flaws. They are the story of a
person who has lived, loved, lost and risen.
My reflection is not something to fix,
it is someone to honour.

I will choose **UNDERSTANDING**,
For my body's wisdom, my skin's signals,
And my heart's longing to feel whole, not hidden.
I will not silence my needs with shame.
I will meet them with nourishment.

I will practice **TRUST**,
In the slow magic of real care,
In the regenerative power of nature and time,
And in my body's ability to restore, rebalance,
and glow again.
Because I am growing and becoming.

And above all, I will remember:
Beauty begins with **YOU**.
Not with products.
Not with procedures.
But with the way you choose to see yourself.

So I choose to see myself through kind eyes, I choose to touch my skin with reverence, and I choose to live today in a body that is not perfect, but is powerfully, beautifully, mine.

BEAUTY WINGS

I met a woman recently who had a deep interest in butterflies. She went on to explain the basics to me... that they start off as caterpillars, eating their way through leaves. They then cocoon themselves and eventually turn into butterflies.

What I didn't know was that to turn from a caterpillar into a butterfly is a feat of nature, a process that takes an extraordinary struggle for the butterfly to break out of the cocoon. But that struggle has a purpose. It strengthens the butterfly's wings so that when it finally breaks free from the cocoon, it is able to fly. She explained to me that if nature had created an easier process for the butterfly its wings would never be strong enough and it would die.

Much like the butterfly, strengthening our own beauty wings is a personal journey that with all its challenges takes us closer to the truth of what makes us beautiful human beings.

This can be confronting and often we look at situations and wonder why things have to be so difficult? Why are so many of us challenged in this area of our lives, never feeling as though we look how we would like to?

My own path through the world has shown me that for most of us there is a certain amount of struggle before we reach a point where we are strong enough to simply be free and fly.

So on those days when you are feeling challenged, for something simple or more significant, try to keep in mind that you are strengthening your beauty wings and getting ready to fly.

Be BEAUTIFUL, Be Free...

AS YOU JOURNEY THROUGH LIFE...

*May you always celebrate and
remember your beauty
May this beauty always dance in the
presence of your love
And may you always nurture the house
That enables you to do this... your heart.*

GREGORY LANDSMAN'S DE-STRESS & AGE LESS™ METHODOLOGY

Gregory Landsman's De-Stress & Age Less Series (*Face Value, Face Fitness, Face Food*), stand at the forefront of psychodermatology; the science that recognises the inextricable link between the mind, emotions, and skin health. Decades before the field became widely acknowledged, Gregory Landsman's work pioneered the integration of stress reduction, nutrition, and topical care to treat skin on every level.

Modern research confirms that chronic stress and elevated cortisol accelerate skin aging, deplete collagen and elastin, impair barrier function, and intensify dryness and inflammation.

This method helps to stop premature skin aging by purging the body from the internal and lifestyle driven stress that create free radicals and destroys the skin's building blocks, collagen and elastin. Dealing with stress fortifies the body's defence system and supports collagen production, which results in healthier, more vital looking skin at every age. It also increases feelings of wellbeing, which means we look better and feel better.

So while traditional beauty regimens focus only on surface correction, Landsman's methodology addresses one of the root causes of skin problems - the way stress imprints on the body and shows itself on the face.

> *When you change the way you breathe, eat cortisol lowering foods, use potent active vitamin rich botanical skincare formulas and stimulate the facial muscles, you will revive, renew and repair your skin... at any age.*

ABOUT THE AUTHOR
GREGORY LANDSMAN PHD

BEST SELLING AUTHOR
GLOBAL BEAUTY & WELLNESS EXPERT
NATURAL SKINCARE PIONEER
TV HOST

*H*aving spent more than 35 years in the global beauty industry Gregory Landsman is one of the most noted beauty and wellness experts in the world, a dry skin expert for women 50+ and a best selling author of ten books.

His science-based approach is used in universities, recommended by doctors and shared with global audiences through his books and TV show *Face Lifting Food*, shown in more than 70 countries worldwide. Gregory Landsman is also the CEO of the GL Skinfit Institute® and the founder of the GL Dissolving Differences Foundation - a not for profit organisation that focusses on education initiatives for youth to overcome body image dissatisfaction.

His work also supports Cancer wellness centres, helping patients to overcome dry skin brought on by medical treatments through natural topical treatments and food choices.

Books by Gregory Landsman include:

- Face Food
- Face Value
- Face Secrets
- Men's Skin Health
- A Lifetime of Beauty
- The Balance of Beauty Explodes the Body Myth

CONNECT WITH GREGORY LANDSMAN

If you would like to hear from me personally with updates, insights, stories and tips on how to de-stress and age less please go to gregorylandsman.com and sign up. I look forward to you joining us.

Gregory Landsman official site:

www.ingramcontent.com/pod-product-compliance
Lightning Source LLC
Chambersburg PA
CBHW050832010526
44110CB00054BA/2656